GETTING TO KNOW

Hackety Hack

DON RAUF

rosen publishing's
rosen central®

NEW YORK

Published in 2015 by The Rosen Publishing Group, Inc.
29 East 21st Street, New York, NY 10010

First Edition

Library of Congress Cataloging-in-Publication Data

Rauf, Don, author.
Getting to know Hackety Hack/Don Rauf.—First edition.
pages cm.—(Code power: a teen programmer's guide)
Audience: Grades 5 to 8.
Includes bibliographical references and index.
ISBN 978-1-4777-7705-3 (library bound)—ISBN 978-1-4777-7707-7 (pbk.)—ISBN 978-1-4777-7708-4 (6-pack)
1. Ruby (Computer program language)—Juvenile literature. 2. Computer programming—Juvenile literature. I. Title.
QA76.73.R83R38 2015
005.13'3--dc23
                                                                    2013044848

Manufactured in the United States of America

{ CONTENTS

>> A "hacker" has great skills at computer programming. Ted Meyer, a student at Worcester Polytechnic Institute, is pictured here sleeping as his team works during a hacking competition.

UCTION

The word "hack" in the world of computers often seems to have a bad meaning. We've all heard the expression "hacking the system." It is often used to describe someone who is illegally using computer code to break into a system that he or she should not be accessing. In the press, hacking frequently means something underhanded and notorious.

But hacking does not have to be synonymous with shady and unethical programming practices. "Cracking the system" may be a more appropriate word for underhanded coding, while all hacking really means is having mad skills at programming. That's why ace programmers wear the title "hacker" as a badge of honor. And that's why Jonathan Gillette, when he created an innovative tool for teaching computer programming, chose the name Hackety Hack.

Hackety Hack is an integrated development environment, or IDE, that lets people interact with and develop computer programs. Like other program environments for beginners, such as Scratch and Alice, Hackety Hack breaks free of the more rigid language structures involved in typical programming. It's meant to make programming fun, rather than intimidating or daunting. In an open letter, Steve Klabnik, who now runs Hackety Hack, wrote: "It's the best way for people who've never learned programming to get their feet wet. It uses Ruby, combined with a GUI [graphical user interface] toolkit named Shoes, to make it really easy to make all kinds of animations, games, and other applications."

Hackety Hack includes a series of interactive lessons that walk the user through some basic commands in the computer language Ruby. It also encourages users to practice making programs using its built-in editor. To facilitate practice, Hackety Hack's website (http://hackety.com) offers tutorials, sample programming code, and forums in which users share the programming codes they've created (http://hackety.com/programs).

Using tools like Hackety Hack to learn programming offers a wide range of benefits. The user finds out how to put mathematics to work in a practical way. Working with code promotes algebraic thinking. The sites that support such programming tools also promote social networking and sharing of ideas. The International Society for Technology in Education says that simple and fun tools like Hackety Hack teach crucial information and communication skills, thinking and problem-solving skills, and interpersonal and self-directional skills. These are all talents that employers look for when hiring. In addition, many top-paying technology-related jobs require computer programming abilities, so it's a terrific skill to start learning now.

Computer code is like any language. It can't really be learned just by reading about it. One must learn by doing. So get to know Hackety Hack and let it guide you into the wide, wondrous world of programming, where the only limits are those of your imagination.

WHY THE LUCKY STIFF

In the world of computer programming, Jonathan Gillette is the stuff of legend. He's in his thirties and has appeared in public unshaven, a bit scruffy, and with long hair. At events, he wears jeans, a T-shirt, and a sports jacket. Many say that he looks like he plays in an indie rock band—and they're right. One of his many creative projects has been making music with a band called the Child Who Was a Keyhole. Gillette, who reportedly comes from Salt Lake City, Utah, is also a prolific writer and cartoonist.

>> He may look like comedian Jack Black or an indie rock star, but Jonathan Gillette (aka "Why the Lucky Stiff") created Hackety Hack, an application designed to teach complete beginners how to program.

WHO IS WHY?!

Gillette is most famous, however, for being a computer programmer who goes by the name "Why the Lucky Stiff" or sometimes just "_why." He uses this identity online, and _why is not a typo. For years, he has tried to keep his real identity a secret. Online searches reveal very little personal information about the notorious, mysterious Jonathan Gillette. When he would attend conferences on computer programming, Gillette would use a pseudonym (a fake name) to register. He'd usually pay his registration fee in cash so as not to reveal his real name by using a credit card. After any public appearance, he

>> A crowd including fifth graders, grad students, professional hackers, and college professors attend "Art && Code," an event devoted to arts-oriented code.

would usually just disappear so that no one could get too close to finding out his true identity.

In the spring of 2009, Gillette made news in the programming world when he presented a speech at Carnegie Mellon University in Pittsburgh, Pennsylvania. He spoke before a room packed with student programmers at an event called "Art && Code," where experts come to discuss arts-oriented programming. His talk was about something he called "The Little Coder's Predicament." The predicament is that we are all surrounded by advanced technologies that require computer programs to operate. Every day we use smartphones, play console games, access websites, and watch videos online. But few of us know the first thing about writing the code needed to make these technologies work.

PROGRAMMING WAS EASIER

Gillette pointed out that some older computers were relatively easy to program. He observes that the Commodore 64, which was popular in the 1980s, was easy to program, as was the Atari 800 computer. Both of these computers used the programming language BASIC. As a result, those who wrote homemade programs for these computers felt empowered and accomplished. "You were part of the movement to help machines sing!" Gillette wrote on his web page. "You were a programmer!"

As Gillette sees things, the problem today is that—despite the proliferation of laptops, tablets, smartphones, game consoles, and other digital devices—young people "have no means of actually deploying or executing the code on their own hardware." The world of computer coding seems shrouded in mystery

>> The Commodore 64 was an early home computer introduced in 1982 by Commodore International. It was easy to program compared with today's home computers.

and inaccessible to the average user. Young people have no idea what the first step is for learning programming. Gillette says that it's almost impossible for someone to consider writing programs that would work on the Xbox, Gameboy, or a PlayStation, for example. And forget about writing code for your Windows computer or Android phone.

So how can young people be shown that not only is programming not impossibly difficult, dry, or dreary, but actually fun, exciting, liberating, empowering, and wildly creative? On his website, Gillette wrote, "You've got to be able to write a single line of code and see a result. We need some instant results to give absolute beginners confidence. Simple methods for sending an e-mail, reading a web page, playing music." This is where Hackety Hack comes in.

A CHALLENGE TO TECH GIANTS

"The Little Coder's Predicament" ends with a proposal to all the big technology companies. Gillette's "Ultimatum" says, "My challenge is to Sony, Nintendo, Microsoft, Apple, and to those who manufacture and develop our interactive technology. Let us interact with these machines more deeply. Provide us a channel for having a dialogue with the entertainment boxes we nurture and care for. I swear to you, the relationship between the public and your product will assuredly blossom."

Gillette finishes by recommending that the titans of technology include an easy-to-use programming language with their products, akin to the BASIC programming language of the Commodore 64 and Atari 800. Gillette envisions a world in which those who buy the electronics can get more involved and interactive with their gadgets and devices, altering and customizing how they operate and what they are programmed to do. Device users will create and modify and come up with new ideas. And Gillette said that this type of empowerment can lead to innovation, which will only further the interests of tech companies in the long run.

FOR THE LOVE OF RUBY

Gillette had already taken a step to solving this youth programmer predicament when he published a guide in 2004 titled *Why's (Poignant) Guide to Ruby*, which is available for free online. Ruby is one of Gillette's favorite computer languages because it's easy to learn and use.

3.

A Quick (and Hopefully Painless) Ride Through Ruby (with Cartoon Foxes)

>> One of Jonathan Gillette's favorite computer languages is Ruby. Before he created Hackety Hack, he published *Why's (Poignant) Guide to Ruby*, an illustrated guide to the programming language that features cartoon foxes, among other whimsical elements.

In an informative article on Slate.com, the writer Annie Lowrey clearly illustrates how Ruby is simpler than some other programming languages. If a person wants the computer to say, "Hello, world!" on the screen, Ruby's program reads: print "Hello, world!" Meanwhile, with Java, the preferred programming language of billions of cell phones, the same code would be:

```
class Hello     {
      public static void main(String args[])     {
         System.out.println("Hello, world!");
      }
}
```

>> *Why's (Poignant) Guide to Ruby* was written in comic form to make it inviting to the general public (especially young people) and to help show that computer programming can be fun.

Without commands written in a computer programming language, a computer or device is a useless object, a piece of hardware that doesn't do anything. When a person learns the programming language, however, he or she can give a computer commands to perform a range of functions. Gillette believes if young people can make computers do what they want, they become more enthusiastic

about and involved in technology. They become more informed consumers. Some will even become innovators who create new and amazing ways to use existing tools and advance technology to the next stage of product evolution and capability.

Gillette's book, which is written in comic book form, was a first step in making programming accessible to the general public, especially young people. With cartoon foxes appearing throughout, his guide to the Ruby programming language is delightful, engaging, and most of all, not intimidating.

>> THE MYSTERY CONTINUES

Just as things began to take off with Hackety Hack, and as more and more young people were learning programming with its help, Gillette disappeared. By the end of 2009, just a few months after his "Little Coder's Predicament" speech at Carnegie Mellon, Gillette was no longer posting online. Many expressed disappointment, confusion, and even anger. Why had _why seemingly deserted the cause?

Those who loved Gillette's mission did not want to see it disappear. So professional programmers set about capturing all of the material posted and generated on the Hackety Hack website and preserving it for the world to use. As a result, Hackety Hack lives on and thrives. Steve Klabnik maintains Hackety.com, complete with the downloadable application and tutorials.

Many in the programming world, though, say that _why is dead—not the real person but the identity he created. Peter Cooper, a programming teacher who runs a Ruby news site, wrote that the character _why met an end, but the person who created and lives behind the character—Gillette—is still out there, although he has disappeared from the programming scene for whatever reason.

Although _why has mysteriously removed himself from the world of programming, his programming tutorial is no mystery. It's still a practical, easy way to learn a simple programming language and discover how to create some basic computer functions in a short amount of time. It encourages the young code writer to achieve ever more accomplished and sophisticated feats of programming.

A MAN OF ACTION

Even though he had presented his *(Poignant) Guide* to the world, Gillette wanted to do more to encourage the efforts of young programmers. He wanted to take concrete action that would produce results. So at the 2005 conference, Gillette introduced a system called Hackety Hack that teaches teens and even younger users how to use the Ruby programming language.

When those who are new to computer programming see the lines and lines of code required to operate even basic functions and tasks, it can make their heads spin. The Hackety Hack application, available free online, is designed to make sense of it by teaching young people how easy it is to use Ruby. As its website says, Hackety Hack teaches the absolute basics of programming from the ground up. No previous programming experience is needed.

Ruby is an open-source programming language. That means it's free for all to use. Its focus is on simplicity and productivity. It is designed to be natural to read and easy to write. In the *(Poignant) Guide*, Gillette claims, "Ruby will teach you to express your ideas through a computer. You will be writing stories for a machine. The language will become a tool for you to better connect your mind to the world."

CHAPTER 2

HACKETY HACK AND RUBY: PERFECT TOGETHER

While Gillette champions the programming language Ruby, and it's at the core of Hackety Hack, where did Ruby itself

come from? Ruby has been ranked as one of the top ten most popular programming languages. Yukihiro Matsumoto ("Matz" for short) created the programming language in 1993. He set out to make a language that's easy to write and practical yet fun to use.

WHAT MAKES RUBY SHINE

As a student of computer programming who was

>> Yukihiro Matsumoto (or "Matz") created the programming language Ruby to be fun and easy to use. True Ruby fans subscribe to the motto "Matz Is Nice, So We Are Nice," or MINSWAN.

fluent in many programming languages, Matz was nevertheless frustrated by existing codes. He wanted the process to be easier and faster. Matz says that his language is simple in appearance but "very complex inside, just like our human body." His goal in creating Ruby was to enhance the programmer's productivity and fun. He wanted programmers to be happy. One thing that makes them especially happy is that, as an open-source language, Ruby is free for all to experiment with and use.

Ruby is object-oriented programming (OOP), as opposed to procedural programming. A procedural program tells a computer what to do with a list of tasks and step-by-step instructions. These languages include C, C++, Fortran, Pascal, and BASIC (although some of these languages can be object-oriented as well). With a procedural program, a person types in the lines of code. With OOP, programming is a collection of interacting "objects" instead of a long list of commands. Each of these objects has a distinct role. An object in an animation program, for example, may tell a character to walk or jump—activities that would otherwise require dozens, even hundreds of lines of procedural programming code.

Matz combined ideas drawn from other programming languages to create Ruby. He drew on the languages Perl, Smalltalk, Eiffel, Ada, and Lisp. When the first version of Ruby was ready in December 1995, Matz released it in his home country of Japan. Until 1999, it pretty much stayed within Japan, but in the meantime, he kept refining the program. When Ruby version 1.3 came out four years after the language's first introduction, the world finally began to take notice.

>> David Heinemeier Hansson came up with a new way to use Ruby called Ruby on Rails (RoR), a web application framework that makes it easier to build an elaborate website.

RUBY ON RAILS

Ruby became widely known when a framework called Ruby on Rails (RoR) was introduced in 2006 but which Matz did not create. Another programmer, the digital entrepreneur David Heinemeier Hansson, took Ruby and came up with this new way to use it. Hansson is a partner in the company Basecamp, which makes software for the web. He is also a racecar driver, photographer, and family man. His company is most known for creating Basecamp, a project management and collaboration application.

RoR reduces the amount of code a person needs to write—a user doesn't have to write certain fundamental code over and over again. RoR speeds website development and makes it easier to build a complex website with apps. Now many types of companies are using it, from small start-ups to multimillion-dollar communications, media, and tech companies. Twitter, Hulu, LivingSocial, Groupon, and the Yellow Pages are using Ruby on Rails for some of their web applications.

>> RUBYISTS ARE NICE!

Rubyists, as those who are true believers in Ruby and worship Matz's creation are referred to, are renowned for being helpful and eager to help those who are ready to learn. They follow the motto "MINSWAN," which is an acronym that stands for "Matz Is Nice, So We Are Nice." They want those who are new to Ruby to be able to use it to tell their stories and express their ideas through the computer. Gillette is one of these Rubyists. The MINSWAN ethos informs his creation of Hackety Hack and the commitment to ease of programming that it fosters.

Anyone can use Ruby on his or her home computer or laptop. Various Ruby-related websites explain how to get started, and an absolute beginner can dive in immediately and use the language to write a computer game or build a program that will solve math problems. The software is available for both Mac and PC.

RUBY IN THE REAL WORLD

As a website programmer at the New York Public Library in New York City, Sean Redmond uses Ruby and Ruby on Rails. He has also used Hackety Hack and read *Why's (Poignant) Guide to Ruby*. Redmond and his team work with RoR on the website MyLibraryNYC.org. A teacher can go to this website and order sets of books for his or her class. The tool for ordering the books is created with Ruby on Rails, and Redmond recommends that interested programmers visit the site to see how Ruby can be used to generate a web page. Redmond had also worked at the

>> Many companies and institutions use Ruby in some way, including Amazon, the BBC, Cisco, IBM, J. P. Morgan, NASA, Yahoo!, and the Guggenheim Museum.

Guggenheim Museum in New York, where staff used Ruby to program the portion of the Guggenheim website that allows users to view the museum's collection online.

When Redmond starts a web project in RoR, he first runs a little program that generates a skeletal website called "scaffolding." This gives him the initial structure upon which he will build what he wants. With the RoR framework, Redmond can build helpful tools for the web page visitor. For example, he can build a tool that allows users to convert a temperature from Fahrenheit to Celsius. The user sees the tool on the screen and can easily type in a temperature and get it converted. Behind the scenes, however, there are lines and lines of code that make that tool operate so quickly and seemingly effortlessly and automatically. "RoR gives you a lot of the utility you're going to need for any website and the ability to make pages that involve users and take input from forms," said Redmond in an interview with the author. "It's actually really pleasant to program in Ruby. Learning is easy because it is consistent. If you learn A, and you learn B, you can probably figure out C for yourself."

Redmond believes that Hackety Hack is a great way to get into the world of Ruby. "Hackety Hack makes it easy to express ideas you might have in a simple way," he said. "The GUI called Shoes makes it fun. Computers are a part of our lives. They should be friendly, and Hackety Hack helps make them friendly."

A person does not necessarily have to be a computer whiz and math genius to get involved in the world of programming. Redmond is a great example of a person who got involved in programming but did not start as a computer programmer. Instead, he had intended to be a teacher. He earned a graduate degree in the classics, a branch of the humanities comprising the languages, literature, philosophy, history, art, and archaeology of ancient Greece and Rome. In grad school, Redmond got involved in a project devoted to the digitizing and managing of all the data associated with a major bibliography. He wanted to make the work of putting together the bibliography easier, and programming was the answer.

Redmond loved teaching Latin classes in grad school, and he sees web programming as an extension of that. "Programming, like teaching, is all about taking the raw material and getting it across to people in some way that they can understand—making it digestible," he said. "When you're teaching a class, you're interfacing with the students, helping them understand something. When you're creating a website or app, you're creating an interface. Teaching and programming are more similar than you think at first."

Redmond believes that a lot of people get into programming because they want something that doesn't exist. "They think it would be great if there were a program or a website or an app that did this," said Redmond, who has also worked as website programmer at the Brooklyn Museum. "These people figure out that they can make it themselves. It becomes a fun thing to do, and then to find out it's useful to other people is even better."

Redmond encourages young people to get involved with programming because so much that they do today involves computers. "If you love video games, it's easy to build one on your computer," he said. "You already have everything you need to get started and get into so many computer fields. If you are playing *Minecraft*, you already have what you need to make the next *Minecraft*. All you need is a computer and your imagination."

HOW TO START HACKETY HACKING

W ithout any programming experience and no matter what age you are, you can start to master programming with the help of Hackety Hack. To start learning how to use the Ruby programming language with Hackety Hack, begin by visiting the website Hackety.com.

COMMANDING THE TURTLE TO DRAW

The next step is to download the Hackety Hack application into the computer, whether it be a Mac or PC. The application icon is a character some call Hackety Mouse (a cartoon icon of a white mouse wearing a red cape—although it also resembles a fox).

After opening the application, a window appears on the computer screen with which the user can interact. In that window sits a small icon—a cartoon turtle holding a pen. The turtle is awaiting

>> Hai-Ri Park, Brett Fernandez, and Payal Khimani work on a computer program during a "hackathon," in which groups of computer scientists create code together during a twenty-four-hour period.

your programming instructions to know what to do. It will sit still, but once it receives the instructions, it springs into action.

To get the turtle going, a user has to click on the editor tab. This is where the turtle receives orders. Hackety Hack asks the first-timer to type "Turtle.draw" in the box that appears. "Turtle" is basically the subject, and "draw" is the verb. The period serves as a connector in this program. Whatever comes after the period is a command telling the subject what to do. After this is typed in, the user can hit the "Run" button, and the turtle is now in the draw mode, ready to draw.

The next learning step is to give the screen a different background. Users are instructed to type in this command:

Turtle.draw do
background maroon
end

Then click "Run," and the background changes color to maroon. Instructions for the computer must be given in a list format. The word "end" signals to the computer that the commands are over.

The instruction guide then kicks it up a notch, asking the user to set the color of the "pen" that the turtle holds. The user

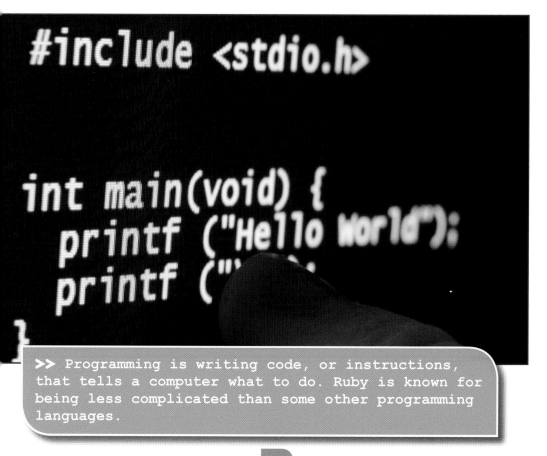

>> Programming is writing code, or instructions, that tells a computer what to do. Ruby is known for being less complicated than some other programming languages.

then also commands the turtle to make a line with the custom-colored pen. The suggested command is:

```
Turtle.draw do
background lightslategray
pencolor honeydew
forward 50
end
```

Three things happen here: The background changes color (to light slate gray), the pen gets a color (honeydew), and the turtle draws a line that is fifty pixels long. (A pixel is basically a point on the computer screen.)

The next programming task to learn is to have the turtle draw a square by having it move forward and make a series of right turns. The command "Turnright 90" gives the direction and the angle (a square has four corners with 90-degree angles). The Hackety Hack tutorial will have you guess how to write the command codes for the turtle to draw a square. Here is one possibility:

```
Turtle.draw do
background lightslategray
pencolor honeydew
forward 50
turnright 90
forward 50
turnright 90
forward 50
```

```
turnright 90
forward 50
end
```

This instructs the turtle to draw a square with sides that are fifty pixels each.

REPEAT, REPEAT

The user can see from the previous examples that programming can involve a lot of repeat instructions. But instead of writing forward 50, turnright 90 four times, there is another, simpler way. The computer can be given instructions to repeat a certain action. In this case, the same square can be drawn with these instructions:

```
Turtle.draw do
background lightslategray
pencolor honeydew
4.times do
forward 50
turnright 90
end
end
```

The computer has been instructed to make a line fifty pixels long, followed by a 90-degree right turn, four times. The end result is a square. The user can now experiment with some other shapes—like triangles or hexagons—by trying different pixel lengths, different angles, and different amounts of repetition (how many times the computer is instructed to repeat a certain action).

HELLO, WORLD!

In its introductory lessons, Hackety Hack tells the user how to program the computer so that desired words appear on the screen. All coding must go through the Editor tool.

For example, to display the words "Hello, world!" the tutorial says to type in:

alert "Hello, world!"

Alert is the verb that tells the computer what to do. In Ruby, this verb is referred to as the "method." This line of programming is instructing the computer to put an alert box on the screen, and the information inside the quotations—in this case, "Hello, world!"—goes in that box.

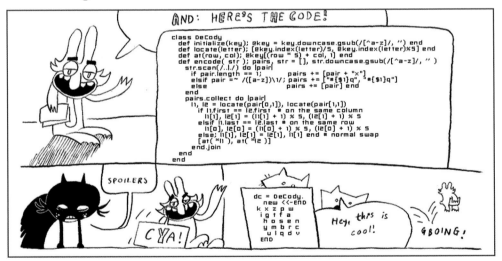

>> For those just starting to program, code might be used to build a simple number-guessing game, tell a knock-knock joke, or have the computer ask you your name. *Why's (Poignant) Guide* provides numerous examples of code that uses the Ruby programming language to tell the computer what to do in certain situations.

BUILDING AN INTERACTIVE PROGRAM

As the beginning lesson moves along, the Hackety Hack user learns more sophisticated techniques. A beginning programmer can establish a way to have the computer ask a person a question that requires an answer. The following line of coding asks a question and brings up a box so that the user can type in an answer:

name = ask "What is your name?"

The user can then type in his or her name. Let's say the person's name is Dave. Follow that previous line of code with:

alert "Hello, " + name

Now the alert will come up "Hello, Dave."

Hackety Hack also shows a user how to build a quiz using programming language. In the tutorial's example, the mini-quiz asks a person to guess a secret number. By writing specific lines of code, the screen will say, "I have a secret number. Take a guess and see if you can figure it out." A box appears on screen where the quiz taker can put in his or her guess. Code is then written that will provide the message "Yes! You guessed right!" whenever someone inputs a correct numerical guess. If the quiz taker guesses wrong, a line of code signals the following message to appear: "Sorry, you'll have to try again."

Of course, a quiz that asks a human to guess a number from one to infinity is super hard on the guesser. After all, what are the odds of getting it right? To make it easier on the quiz taker, a few easy lines of instructions can help. After the answer line, the computer can be instructed to tell the quiz taker: "Too high" or "Too low."

Once a new programmer masters a simple quiz like this, he or she may want to code a knock-knock joke. Knock-knock jokes are fun and they follow a predictable pattern, so coding is fairly easy. Here's an example:

Computer: Knock, knock
Human: Who's there?
Computer: Cowp
Human: Cowp Who?
Computer: Cow poo? Gross!

PUT YOURSELF IN THESE SHOES

Hackety Hack works with a graphical user interface toolkit called Shoes. A graphical user interface, or GUI (pronounced gooey), is basically all the elements you see on a screen to help you navigate and accomplish all you want with a computer. Shoes runs on Microsoft Windows, Mac OS X, and Linux.

A GUI may have windows, icons, and menus indicating where to click and access applications and information. The graphic aspect makes it easier to accomplish tasks. With a GUI, a person may be able to download an application and simply slide an icon into an app folder to have that application begin to work. The alternative would be typing in commands to accomplish the

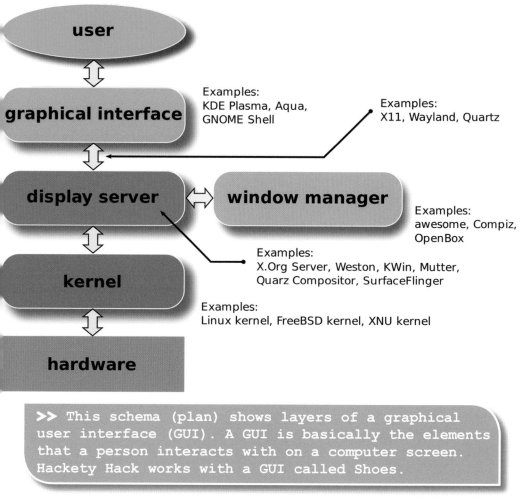

>> This schema (plan) shows layers of a graphical user interface (GUI). A GUI is basically the elements that a person interacts with on a computer screen. Hackety Hack works with a GUI called Shoes.

same thing, which would be cumbersome, time consuming, and error-prone.

Shoes also makes it possible to put a graphic button on the screen. The GUI user can click on the button to get information, submit information, or carry out a task. A person can insert titles, graphics, illustrations, and photos. A video can be placed on the page, which either starts right away or after a user clicks on it. Shoes provides an easy way to provide animation on a website. Those just beginning to use Shoes might find

>> SOME KEY LINGO

As a person learns the ropes of programming, some common phrases are used to describe different elements. Here are a few that should help the beginner:

Strings: Strings are groups of characters or words that a programmer types between quotation marks. The words will appear on the screen to the user. By typing in: alert "Hello, how are you?" the computer is commanded to display "Hello, how are you?" on the screen.

Method: In Ruby, verbs or commands are called methods. If a user types in the word "alert," for example, that verb tells the computer to create a box on the screen, and whatever string follows will go in the box. So if a person types alert "Hello, how are you?" then that text within the quotations appears in a box on the screen.

Array: An array is a collection, group, or list of data or variables. It could be a list of names, for example. An array could be described as a variable that holds multiple pieces of data. Brigham Young University provides a great tutorial on arrays. The lesson explains how arrays use compartments to hold information. A search engine may use an array to store web pages found when a user performs a search.

Variable: This is a piece of information. A variable can equal something. The variable could be hotdogs = 5. This is called an assignment. Variables are often-used items.

Shell: We all know a snail has a shell, as does an egg, but computer programming also has shells. A shell is a software program that can translate the commands given by a user so that the operating system of the computer can understand them and then carry out the directions.

a picture online or from their own picture folder and display it in the GUI.

A good exercise is to use Shoes to incorporate interactive elements, such as a space where users can enter their name. Once the user enters a name in that field and hits enter, program commands can instruct the computer to then display text that reads "Hello, [Person's Name]!"

As one gets more familiar with Shoes, the GUI can get more elaborate. A common method to interact with a screen is with stacks and flows. Stacks are vertical lines of boxes that a user may click on or scroll over to get more information, submit information, or complete a task. Flows are similar, but they run horizontally instead of vertically. Look at a Google search page, for example, and notice that a stack is on the left that allows the user to search the web, images, videos, news, shopping, etc. The flow on a page may offer boxes to click through to search the web, browse images, gain access to e-mail, consult a calendar, etc.

The only real way to learn about Shoes is to dig in and try it. The Shoes website provides a lot of helpful information to guide one's beginning efforts (www.shoesrb.com). The Shoes Manual at this site gives a quick walk-through of how it works.

CHAPTER 4

LOOK WHAT I MADE!

Many of us know how to use the Internet, open a Word document, and maybe play a game on our computers. But very few actually know how to create a game for their computers or build programs that can add or do simple math.

With the help of Hackety Hack, people from around the world have been able to make their own programs—from a simple game of *Pong* to a calendar/clock application. Simple programs have been developed for solving math equations and presenting question-and-answer formats. The Hackety Hack site provides a section that includes the codes and programs created by ordinary users. For example, there's a *Space Invaders* game and Connect Four. There's a program that plays "Happy Birthday." There is a short program that asks the user to confirm if Devin is smelly. If the user enters "true," then the text "He sure is smelly" appears.

ONE STEP BEYOND

While Hackety Hack will get students to begin coding with the programming language Ruby, it's also worth visiting TryRuby.org to get some basic experience. The site is a tribute to *Why's (Poignant) Guide to Ruby*, so it adopts Gillette's unique style (including

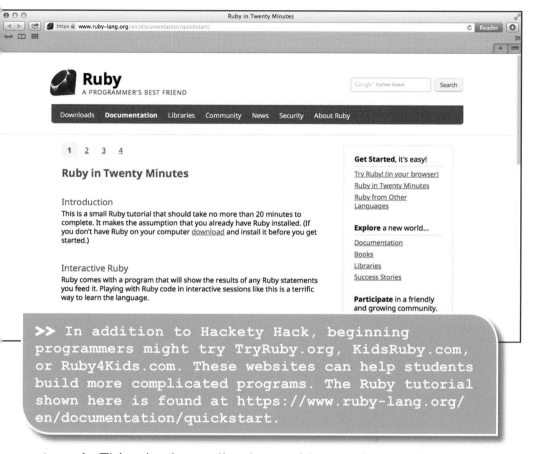

>> In addition to Hackety Hack, beginning programmers might try TryRuby.org, KidsRuby.com, or Ruby4Kids.com. These websites can help students build more complicated programs. The Ruby tutorial shown here is found at https://www.ruby-lang.org/en/documentation/quickstart.

cartoons). This site immediately provides an interactive window that shows how some simple programming works. The user first has to type in the word "help" to get things rolling.

Ruby recognizes numbers and math symbols, so the first interaction is to try some basic math—addition, subtraction, multiplication, and division. Put in 6 * 4, and up pops => 24. Another tutorial shows you how to type in a string that spells your name, and then a method is in place to reverse the spelling of your name. So if one types in "David".reverse, up pops divaD. The method is the action after the period ("reverse"); without it, the computer doesn't know what to do.

On TryRuby.org, the beginner learns how to store information between brackets and then manipulate the input with a method. The user is prompted to put three numbers between the brackets—[12, 47, 35]—followed by .max. That method tells the computer to pick the highest number in the series.

The tutorial also shows exactly how to create a variable. The variable is called "ticket" in the mini-lesson, and the three numbers 12, 47, and 35 are placed within that variable. If the user types in "ticket" after setting this up, the computer knows to use those three numbers. So by typing in "ticket.sort," the computer takes the three numbers and follows the command or method to sort. On screen appears [12, 35, 47], sorted by increasing value. As the lesson goes on, the user finds that information in brackets can be swapped out using an equals sign. A poem is presented about toast going to the moon, but when the direction poem['toast']='honey¬dew' is given, the toast becomes honeydew.

Another website, KidsRuby.com, features a lot of feedback and ideas from young Rubyists. Plus, the site offers listings of conferences and camps that kids can attend; notices of special programming-related events; and information on available classes, lectures, and exercises.

Ruby4Kids.com is similarly useful and instructive. This site demonstrates how to write the code to build a game called *Falling Blocks* (similar to *Tetris*). It also provides a link to *Gosu*, a 2-D game development library. The site provides "building blocks" to create games—chunks of programming code that can make creating a game easier. One of the components offered is a main loop—a repeating piece of code that carries out a main task.

>> A GATEWAY TO GAME DEVELOPMENT

Building a game can get fairly complex, and a lot of elements have to come together and work correctly in response to a player's commands and responses—establishing players, keyboard and gamepad input, movement methods, animation, text, sounds, and more.

Building games is complicated and takes time, but it can be done. For inspiration, check out the website of *Gosu*, a 2-D game development library for the Ruby and C++ programming languages (www.libgosu.org). Here, people who are creating their own games trade opinions and share programming ideas that can improve each other's games.

Gosu's site features zombie-themed games, space shooters, Captain Ruby, Futurecop, the *Legend of Purple Dot*, and games where you make hamburgers. In one game, the player has to pilot a submarine to the bottom of the ocean before the music ends. Another game is Gagalaxies, a single-player sci-fi strategy game that focuses on decision making, rather than empire building. The game revolves around different strategies that the player can select at the beginning of each turn and that determine his order of play.

On Gosu, game creators provide notes on glitches and problems. Sometimes programmers making Ruby-based games will post YouTube videos that demonstrate exactly how their games move and operate. Seeing how others make their games can provide you with the inspiration and programming smarts necessary to make your own.

Ruby4Kids also offers game designers code callback functions. These are mechanisms that wait for events to occur. They will call selected functions in response to particular events. For example, a callback may be triggered by clicking on a button, filling out certain information, or taking a player to the next level of a game after completing specific tasks. Ruby4Kids also gives game-builders 2-D graphics and text, as well as sound samples and music.

OTHER WAYS TO START PROGRAMMING

While Hackety Hack offers a great launching pad into the world of programming, there are a few other ways to explore and learn the mysteries of coding. Here are some of the tools that let beginners dip their toes into programming, without any prior coding knowledge or experience. These gateway tools can open the doors to more elaborate and sophisticated programming. They all offer simple methods for organizing coded instructions for the computer.

SCRATCH

The Massachusetts Institute of Technology (MIT) Media Lab came up with a programming language designed to show young people how to animate and make games. As the MIT website explains, Scratch is designed to help young people "think creatively, reason systematically, and work collaboratively." Since it came out in 2007, the program has been wildly popular. There are more than eight hundred thousand users and more than one million projects posted on the site. It's being used in more than 150 countries, and the Media Lab said that more than 1,500 games and animation projects are uploaded every day.

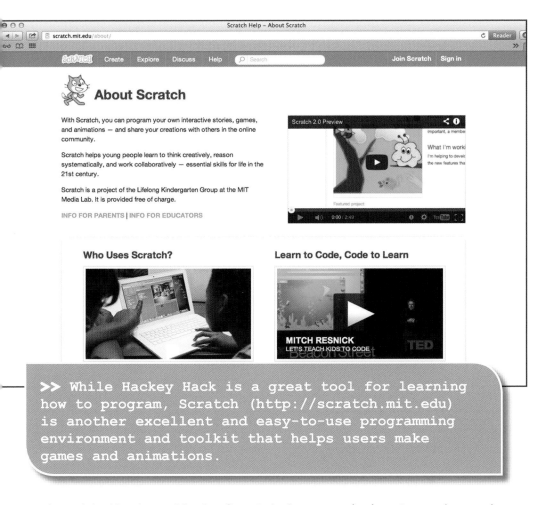

>> While Hackey Hack is a great tool for learning how to program, Scratch (http://scratch.mit.edu) is another excellent and easy-to-use programming environment and toolkit that helps users make games and animations.

As with Hackety Hack, Scratch has a mission to make coding simple—even those in fourth and fifth grade can construct the programming for a project. Through Scratch, a person drags instructions in pieces and drops them into a framework to show what actions should be happening on the screen and in what order. The actions are easily rearranged by clicking and dragging elements with the mouse. Some compare the Scratch programming experience to playing with blocks or placing jigsaw puzzle pieces.

ALICE

Alice is another super-easy, user-friendly system with which to learn programming. Alice teaches in a visual way, so the new programmer can watch what his or her program does. It is a free, object-based programming language, founded by Randy Pausch, who unfortunately died of pancreatic cancer in 2008. (Pausch gave an upbeat talk at Carnegie Mellon University in 2007 called "The Last Lecture: Really Achieving Your Childhood Dreams," which went on to become the basis for a top-selling book.)

Alice couples a drag-and-drop editor with characters and ani-

mated action. A student can make his or her own animated movies and simple video games in a 3-D virtual environment. The instructions that one creates in Alice are similar to ones a programmer would create in languages such as Java, C++, and C#. The training one acquires through Alice can gradually shift over to these other more widely used languages. The drag-and-drop

>> Randy Pausch, a former University of Virginia professor who died of cancer in 2008, helped create Alice, another user-friendly system for learning how to program.

technique eliminates the possibility of making errors when typing in code.

Combining the coding with animation, Alice lets the programmer see immediately how the code is working. If a student places code to make a character move right but the character moves left, he or she can see the mistake instantly on the screen. The newest version, Alice 3.0, lets the user switch between programming with the drag-and-drop system and Java programming code. Through a partnership with the huge game maker Electronic Arts (EA), Alice has incorporated characters and actions from the widely popular game *The Sims 2*.

ARDUINO

This programming language may not be as simple to learn as Hackety Hack, Alice, or Scratch, but it's still designed to be fairly easy. Arduino calls itself an "open-source electronics prototyping platform" based on flexible, easy-to-use hardware and software. It's intended for artists, designers, hobbyists, and anyone interested in creating interactive objects or environments.

If one goes online and searches for Arduino projects, many video clips of amazing and fun gadgets, toys, tools, and robots appear. One baker built an Arduino device that sends a tweet to customers notifying them when fresh-baked goods have just come out of the oven. Another Arduino project constructed electronic dice. With a push of the button, a random choice between 1 and 6 appears on an LED screen. Using Arduino, you can build a battery tester, a traffic light, and a GPS system.

>> Zlata Barshteyn and Jenny Jiao Hsia collaborate during a game development event. Hackety Hack and similar tools are designed to encourage young people—especially women, who are underrepresented in the field—to get involved in programming.

Arduino was developed by a group of five engineers and artists (mostly based in Italy). It is both something physical (the hardware or tiny programmable computer that can make a gadget operate) and a programming language (the software that gives the instructions for the device to operate). Hardware costs money, but Arduino components are affordable, with a unit costing around $30. A person can dream up ideas for using the system and then bring those ideas to life. It teaches the fundamentals of electronics.

One of the attractive features of Arduino is that it can operate a gadget using sensory information. Sensors that detect light, sound, and temperature can be incorporated into a device and react. That's

>> Lego Mindstorms is a series of kits that include both software and hardware and allow users to create small programmable robots. It's a simple way for young people to learn programming and see their efforts set into motion.

how Puff works. Puff is a small robot dragon on wheels that can sense a heat source, head toward it, and then blow out the flame.

LEGO MINDSTORMS

Like Arduino, Lego Mindstorms is an introduction to the world of robot-building. Like Scratch, it originated in the MIT Media Lab. It comes equipped with a graphical programming language, and users can move around blocks of programming language by clicking and dragging. If a student wants to use another language (Java or Lua, for example), that's possible. Lego also sells robotic kits that can cost hundreds of dollars.

TAKING IT FURTHER

As Steve Klabnik (who took over Hackety Hack after Gillette abandoned it) said, Hackety Hack is a great way to get your toes wet in the world of programming. By learning Ruby through Hackety Hack, a person gets to know how data needs to be structured, what controls are involved, and designs. But to build on these newly acquired programming abilities and techniques, the novice needs to explore other programming languages and methods.

LOOK TO YOUR DESKTOP

Automating actions on your desktop can be a helpful next step. Windows and Mac typically come equipped with programs (AutoHotkey for Windows and Automator for Mac). These tools can automatically rename files and remind you of events like birthdays.

Through Automator, a user can program an action that automatically gives a reminder of upcoming birthdays by placing a text file containing the important dates on the desktop. To do so, one may drag and drop actions into Workflow:

- Find People with Birthdays
- Get Contact Information
- New Text File

In the "Find People with Birthdays" action, one may click "This Week" from the drop-down menu. In the "Get Contact Information" area, check "First Name," "Last Name," and "Birthday" from the list on the left-hand side of the action. Lastly, mark the "Combine Names" checkbox. Through these actions, a person is programming his or her computer to find birthdays and provide a list of those that are coming up in the week ahead.

ENTER THE WORLD OF THE WORLDWIDE WEB

Building a website can be a terrific way to learn programming and coding. The first tool to learn in website building is HTML, or hypertext markup language. Mount Holyoke College posts instructions on how one can learn the fundamentals of HTML in just twenty minutes.

HTML is the language used to build websites. To make the page look attractive, a web designer usually uses CSS (Cascading Style Sheets), which provide the instructions and specifications regarding how the HTML should look on screen. These are not generally considered programming languages but simply ways to structure and style web pages. Still, the principle behind both HTML and CSS is similar to programming.

A next step may be to learn JavaScript, which is the world's most popular programming language and allows users to work with a website. This language is built into all major web browsers, and it makes web pages interactive. It can also be used to create polls and quizzes that can appear on the website.

As with a lot of Ruby programming code, a website builder can find a large amount of preexisting code on the Internet. These chunks of code can be easily copied and pasted into a person's web page to create a desired interactive element. Take a site like Greasemonkey, for example. Here, small bits of JavaScript can help customize the way a web page displays or behaves. HTML basically creates the static framework of a web page, and then JavaScript creates and programs the dynamic elements that perform tasks. All the major web browsers use JavaScript, including Netscape Navigator, Microsoft Internet Explorer, Firefox, Safari, Opera, and Google Chrome.

>> JavaScript is a computer programming language often used for building websites. Also used with PCs, laptops, tablets, and phones, JavaScript has been called the world's most popular programming language. An example of JavaScript code is seen here.

DIVING DEEPER IN PROGRAMMING WATERS

The functions on some websites get more complicated, requiring the use of other programming languages. Ruby can perform some of these functions, but check out the languages PHP, Python, and Perl as well. If users log in to your website and store their personal information there and periodically need to update that information, programming with these more sophisticated languages is required. Tutorials are available on the Internet. Webmonkey is one service that provides solid basic training in these languages.

To learn programming for the web, a person should construct his or her own site. To immerse oneself in this project, it's a good idea to find an idea for a website that one is passionate about. Adam Pash, who had no prior experience making web sites, had an idea for a site where people could quickly create and share music playlists with friends. In one year, he went from a half-baked idea to a fully functioning website called MixTape.me. He said that one of the keys to building the site was that he had a goal and a good idea. He recommends setting time apart from all the other activities of the day to devote to your web design project.

Pash used Ruby on Rails for his framework and a JavaScript library called Prototype. Pash wanted to stream MP3s, so he needed to embed a Flash Player that would allow people to listen to the music. He made a lot of mistakes along the way, but he didn't give up. Learning programming takes patience.

>> Learning how to program can open the doors to many successful and high-paying careers. Here, Jimmy Wales *(left)* founder of Wikipedia, listens to a young programmer describe his work.

Pash realized, too, that while he was doing some programming and learning about it, a lot of the heavy lifting had already been done for him. He was picking up preexisting chunks of open-source code provided by generous developers and simply putting them in place.

KILLER APPS

Apps for mobile phones are hugely popular. Apple's App Store has more than nine hundred thousand apps available and has surpassed a whopping fifty billion downloads. Some of the most popular apps are Pandora Radio and MLB.com At Bat (which lets

>> THE DOWNSIDE OF HACKETY HACK

As with almost every product in the world, Hackety Hack doesn't please everyone. Critics say that with just four lessons and a limited range of examples, Hackety Hack is too superficial and basic. There are no error messages that come up. Some find that it crashes easily. A CommonSenseMedia.org user says, "The content is generally helpful, but kids don't get individual instruction. A clearer connection to math concepts and the addition of other interactive items would make Hackety Hack a stronger learning tool." Users have to know that Hackety Hack will introduce them to the world of programming and get them started, but they will need to dig much deeper and venture farther afield to learn higher-level programming skills and applications.

you watch the MLB.TV baseball *Game of the Day* for free). But the most popular apps, by far, are games—*Minecraft Pocket Edition*, *The Simpsons*, *The Hobbit*, *Kingdoms of Camelot*, *Hay Day*, *Marvel War of Heroes*, *Clash of Clans*, and *Candy Crush*. There are also popular phone apps for Facebook, Twitter, Foursquare, movie show times, restaurant reviews, Groupon, Yelp, the *New York Times*, and many other services. There are apps that can help you locate a parking space, find an ideal date, count calories, learn languages, and create and stick to a budget.

Learning to program for apps takes a high level of knowledge. To scratch the surface and find out some basics about app programming, there are tutorials available online. While

>> Programming skills are essential to build apps for cell phones. Dennis Ai, a student at Northwestern University and founder of Jivehealth, helped develop this app that encourages healthy eating habits in children.

programming is getting easier to learn, especially with guides like Hackety Hack, it can still be frustrating. A lot of trial and error is involved. A programmer should be someone who loves solving problems and gets gratification from little victories. As with anything, the more one practices programming, the easier it gets. Stick with it through the rough patches early on, and the process will soon get easier and more fulfilling.

ANDROID A smartphone (a cell phone that includes software functions such as e-mail and Internet browser) that operates on Google's open-source operating system. All of the major cell phone carriers offer Android phones.

CALLBACK A piece of computer code that is called up by another function.

CASCADING STYLE SHEETS (CSS) A tool used to define the look and feel of web pages. Often web designers will use HTML to mark up content and CSS for design and layout. HTML without CSS is akin to the functional skeleton of the website.

FLASH Animation software, originally developed by Macromedia, that became widely used by the 1990s. Flash animation files are relatively small, so they can be quickly loaded and viewed on slower Internet connections. They are often used on websites.

FLOWS In Hackety Hack, flows are the counterpart to stacks. Instead of going up and down vertically, flows are an organizational system of widgets that runs sideways, or horizontally.

GRAPHICAL USER INTERFACE (GUI) GUI, often pronounced "gooey," provides the visual components that let a person use and interact with a computer. For example, GUIs feature menus, which are drop-down lists of commands from which to choose.

HACK To use or program a computer skillfully; often used (some say incorrectly) as a verb to describe the gaining of illegal access to a computer system or network.

HYPERTEXT MARKUP LANGUAGE (HTML) The language used to create documents and web pages on the World Wide Web. It was developed by scientist Tim Berners-Lee in 1990. HTML tells the browser how to display graphics and text.

JAVA A high-level programming language created by Sun Microsystems that is used primarily for incorporating small programs into pages on the World Wide Web.

JAVASCRIPT With the prefix Java, one might think JavaScript is related to Java, but this is an entirely different programming language. Developed by Netscape, it is the world's most popular programming language and is built into all major web browsers, including Internet Explorer, Firebox, and Safari. JavaScript performs dynamic tasks, like creating a website's polls and quizzes.

LINUX Linux is an operating system for a computer, like Microsoft Windows or Mac OS X. Distributed for free (open source), Linux works on PCs, laptops, mobile and tablet devices, video game consoles, and more. Linux has a reputation for being fast-performing and efficient.

LOOP A fundamental programming idea in which a sequence of instructions is continuously repeated.

LUA A powerful, fast, embeddable scripting language, designed, implemented, and maintained by a team at the Pontifical Catholic University of Rio de Janeiro in Brazil. It is used in games such as *World of Warcraft* and *Angry Birds*.

MP3 Short for Motion Pictures Expert Group Audio Layer 3, an MP3 is a computer file format for compressing and storing digital audio data.

OBJECT–ORIENTED PROGRAMMING (OOP) An object-oriented programming, or OOP, language focused on data and organizing information. Other computer languages, like Fortran, are procedural and focus on commands, telling the computer to "do this" or "do that." OOP languages let people build on instructions that have already been developed, rather than starting from scratch. In OOP, data and functions get put together and are called "objects." OOP languages are easy to modify. Programmers can take existing "objects" and change their features, thereby elaborating on what already exists.

OPEN SOURCE A computer program that provides free access to source code for the general public to use and even modify. Software developers who support open-source code believe that if anyone is interested in modifying computer code, they should be able to, and this type of crowdsourcing will lead to an improved code with fewer mistakes.

PERL Perl is a programming language with the motto, "There's more than one way to do it." It's flexible, evolving, and open source. Its acronym stands for Practical Extraction and Report Language. It is easily able to open and manipulate many files from within the same program.

PHP An open-source, general-purpose scripting language. It is used to enhance web pages. It can be used to create username and password login pages, check details from a form, and create picture galleries and surveys.

PYTHON An interactive, object-oriented programming language that is free to use. It was named after the British comedy troupe Monty Python's Flying Circus. Many components of Google are written in Python, as are the games *Battlefield 2*, *Star Trek Bridge Commander*, and *Civilization 4*.

RUBY ON RAILS Sometimes just called Rails, Ruby on Rails is an open-source web application framework that was built with the programming language Ruby by David Heinemeier Hansson. Some compare Rails to a set of train tracks that smoothly guides you through the process of developing web applications. It incorporates Ruby with HTML, CSS, and JavaScript. Ruby is known among programmers for being a terse, uncluttered programming language that doesn't require a lot of extra punctuation.

STACK A data structure in computer programming where, when a new item is entered in a stack, it is placed on top of all the previous items—just like a stack of cards. When removing an item or object from a stack, the last one in on the top gets removed first. The term LIFO (last in, first out) may be used to refer to this system. In Hackety Hack, it's a way to organize widgets by stacking them on top of each other.

Association of Information Technology Professionals (AITP)
330 North Wabash Avenue, Suite 2000
Chicago, IL 60611-4267
(800) 224-9371
Website: http://www.aitp.org
This worldwide society of professionals in information technology offers career training, scholarships, news, and social networking opportunities.

Canadian Advanced Technology Alliance (CATA)
207 Bank Street, Suite 416
Ottawa, ON K2P 2N2
Canada
(613) 236-6550
Website: http://www.cata.ca
The largest high-tech association in Canada, the CATA is a comprehensive resource for the latest high-tech news in Canada.

National Association of Programmers (NAP)
P.O. Box 529
Prairieville, LA 70769
Website: http://www.napusa.org
This group is dedicated to providing information and resources to help programmers, developers, consultants, and students in the computer industry.

OpenMedia
1424 Commercial Drive

P.O. Box 21674
Vancouver, BC V5L 5G3
Canada
(604) 633-2744
Website: http://openmedia.ca
OpenMedia is a Canadian grassroots organization that safe-
guards the possibilities afforded by a free and open Internet.

TryComputing.org
445 Hoes Lane
Piscataway, NJ 08854-4141
(732) 981-0060
Website: http://www.trycomputing.org/inspire/
computing-student-opportunities
This site hosted by the Institute of Electrical and Electronics
Engineers features competitions, events, internships, and
research programs for young people. It also includes information about career opportunities and colleges with
computer programming courses.

WEBSITES

Due to the changing nature of Internet links, Rosen Publishing
has developed an online list of websites related to the subject of
this book. This site is updated regularly. Please use this link to
access the list:

http://www.rosenlinks.com/CODE/Hack

{FOR FURTHER READING

Brennan, Patricia. *Who Is Bill Gates?* New York, NY: Grosset & Dunlap, 2013.

Briggs, Jason. *Python for Kids*. San Francisco, CA: No Starch Press, 2012.

Crowder, David. *Building a Web Site for Dummies*. Hoboken, NJ: Wiley Publishing, 2010.

Doctorow, Cory. *Little Brother*. New York, NY: Macmillan, 2008.

Farrell, Mary. *Computer Programming for Teens*. Boston, MA: Thomas Course Technology, 2008.

Ford, Jerry Lee. *Programming for the Absolute Beginner* (No Experience Required). Boston, MA: Thomson Course Technology, 2007.

Freedman, Jeri. *Careers in Computer Science and Programming*. New York, NY: Rosen Classroom, 2011.

Frieder, Ophir. *Computer Science Programming Basics in Ruby*. Sebastapol, CA: O'Reilly Media, 2013.

Goldsworthy, Steve. *Steve Jobs* (Remarkable People). New York, NY: AV2 by Weigl, 2011.

Grant, Michael. *BZRK*. New York, NY: Egmont, 2012.

Ivester, Mark. *lol...OMG! What Every Student Needs to Know About Online Reputation Management, Digital Citizenship, and Cyberbullying*. Reno, NV: Serra Knight Publishing, 2011.

Lead Project. *Super Scratch Programming Adventure! Learn to Program by Making Cool Games*. San Francisco, CA: No Starch Press, 2012.

Lloyd, Ian. *Build Your Own Web Site the Right Way Using HTML & CSS*. 2nd ed. Collingwood, Australia: SitePoint, 2008.

Lusted, Marcia Amidon. *Mark Zuckerberg: Facebook Creator* (Essential Lives). Edina, MN: Abdo Publishing Company, 2012.

Lusted, Marcia Amidon. *Social Networking: MySpace, Facebook, & Twitter* (Technology Pioneers). Edina, MN: ABDO Publishing, 2012.

Marques, Marcelo. *Hackerteen: Volume 1: Internet Blackout*. Sebastopol, CA: O'Reilly Media, 2009.

Pine, Chris. *Learn to Program Second Edition* (The Facets of Ruby). Frisco, TX: Pragmatic Bookshelf, 2009.

Robbins, Jennifer Nierderst. *Learning Web Design: A Beginner's Guide to HTML, CSS, JavaScript, and Web Graphics*. Sebastapol, CA: O'Reilly Media, 2012.

Sande, Warren, and Carter Sande. *Hello World! Computer Programming for Kids and Other Beginners*. Greenwich, CT: Manning, 2009.

Sethi, Maneesh. *Game Programming for Teens*. Boston, MA: Thomson Course Technology, 2009.

Applied Sciences Foundation. "Five Tools to Introduce Programming to Kids." Retrieved October 2013 (http://appliedsciencesfoundation.org/?p=923).

BFOIT.org. "Arrays." Retrieved October 2013 (http://www.bfoit.org/itp/Arrays.html).

Brigham Young University. "Intro to Arrays in LiveCode." Retrieved October 2013 (http://revolution.byu.edu/arrays/introToArrays.php).

Cordell, Ryan. "More Hackety Hack, Less Yackety Yack: Ruby for Humanists." *Chronicle of Higher Education*, February 1, 2011. Retrieved October 2013 (http://chronicle.com/blogs/profhacker/more-hackety-hack-less-yackety-yack-ruby-for-humanists/30175).

Dawson, Christopher. "Scratch...Programming for Dummies or a Solid Intro to Object Orientation?" ZDNet, May 18, 2007. Retrieved October 2013 (http://www.zdnet.com/blog/education/scratch-programming-for-dummies-or-a-solid-intro-to-object-orientation/1056).

Easy as Pi Programming. "How Enticing Is Programming?" April 1, 2012. Retrieved October 2013 (http://506raspberrypi.wordpress.com/tag/hackety-hack).

Finley, Klint. "Learn to Program with Hackety Hack." Readwrite.com, January 15, 2011. Retrieved October 2013 (http://readwrite.com/2011/01/15/learn-to-program-with-hackety#awesm=~on6YBDvuDwu5tH).

Friedman, Shay. "IronRuby Unleashed." *Code Magazine*. Retrieved October 2013 (http://www.code-magazine.com/Article.aspx?quickid=100063).

Hackety.com. "Hackety Hack!" Retrieved October 2013 (http://hackety.com).

Harris, Andy. "Exploring Programming with Hackety Hack." SchoolHouseTeachers.com. Retrieved October 2013 (http://schoolhouseteachers.com/2012/09/exploring-programming-with-hackety-hack).

Lardinois, Frederic. "After Disappearing for More Than 3 Years, Why the Lucky Stiff Returns to the Internet." TechCrunch, January 6, 2013. Retrieved October 2013 (http://techcrunch.com/2013/01/06/after-disappearing-for-more-than-3-years-why-the-lucky-stiff-returns-to-the-internet).

Lowrey, Annie. "Where's _why? What Happened When One of the World's Most Unusual, and Beloved, Computer Programmers Disappeared." *Slate*, March 15, 2012. Retrieved October 2013 (http://www.slate.com/articles/technology/technology/2012/03/ruby_ruby_on_rails_and_why_the_disappearance_of_one_of_the_world_s_most_beloved_computer_programmers_.html).

Prillo, Chris. "Would You Like to Be a Hacker, Like in the Movies?" Chris.Pirillo.com. Retrieved October 2013 (http://chris.pirillo.com/would-you-like-to-be-a-hacker-like-in-the-movies).

Ruby4Kids.com. "Ruby for Kids." Retrieved October 2013 (http://ruby4kids.com/ruby4kids).

Ruby-Lang.org. "Ruby: A Programmer's Best Friend." Retrieved October 2013 (https://www.ruby-lang.org/en). Shoes.com.

"Shoes." Retrieved October 2013 (http://shoesrb.com/walkthrough.html).

Technogenous.com. "Computer Programming Resources for
    Kids." October 14, 2012. Retrieved October 2013 (http://
    www.technogeno.us/2012/10/14/computer-programming
    -resources-for-kids). TryRuby.org.
"Try Ruby." Retrieved October 2013 (http://tryruby.org).
Zetcode.com. "Arrays in Ruby." Retrieved October 2013 (http://
    zetcode.com/lang/rubytutorial/arrays).

{ INDEX

ABOUT THE AUTHOR

Don Rauf has a passion for new technology. He was editor of the e-newsletter *Student Health 101*, which features many cutting-edge interactive elements and videos. He also authored *Killer Lipstick and Other Spy Gadgets*; *Perry Chen, Yancey Strickler, Charles Adler, and Kickstarter*; and *A Teen's Guide to the Power of Social Networking*. He has cowritten several books with his wonderful wife, Monique Vescia.

PHOTO CREDITS

Designer: Nicole Russo; Photo Researcher: Cindy Reiman